IT IS ONE of the ironies of American history that the Democratic Party has managed to pass itself off as the champion of the underdog and the crusader for equal rights. The actual history of the Democratic Party – distinct from the history of some individual Democrats – tells a very different story. It is a history in which the lust for power, not a concern for the poor and dispossessed, looms large. *This* story is seldom told. Indeed, so successful has been the suppression of the true history of the Democratic Party for the sake of the "narrative" that simply laying out the facts appears as a startling forensic exercise, a brief for the prosecution. It might begin like this:

Ladies and gentlemen of the jury: I come not to praise the Accused but to bury him. For too long, he has afflicted our body Politic with vilenesses various, seducing our Youth and employing the Institutions of our Government against the People in a nake Quest for Power. For too long, the Enemy has skulked and lurked under cover of good Intentions, subverting the Principles of Self-Reliance, personal Industry, and limited

Government in favor of an alien Ideology whose maleficent and baleful Presence continues to distress our Nation.

A decent respect to the opinions of mankind, therefore, demands this Indictment. The history of the present Democratic Party is a history of repeated injuries and usurpations, all having in direct object the establishment of an absolute Tyranny over the several States. It is, in fact, a criminal Organization masquerading as a political Party.

To prove this, let Facts be submitted to a candid world:

THE ARGUMENT

The first thing you need to know about the Democratic Party is that its first vice president, the traitor Aaron Burr, shot and killed one of the Founding Fathers, Alexander Hamilton, and then plotted sedition against his own president. Everything else is, as they say, commentary.

Again, let me acknowledge that my indictment of the Democratic Party is not necessarily an indictment of individual Democrats, many of whom throughout our history have been true American patriots who worked hard to better the estate of their fellow man. My brief is against the Democratic Party,

---

From the inception of the Republic, the Democratic Party has been a public enemy — an organization antithetical to our nation's traditions, civic virtues, and moral values.

---

which from the inception of the Republic has been a public enemy — an organization antithetical to our nation's traditions, civic virtues, and moral values.

Does that seem overstated? Consider the facts. Whether it has been defending slavery, selling out our secrets, or simply voting "present" so as not to take a stand on the crucial moral issues of both statecraft and soulcraft, the party of slavery, segregation, secularism, and sedition has always been in the forefront of everything inimical to the United States of America.

Its unofficial modern slogan – "by any means necessary" – is indicative of its fundamental amorality. Its will to power, especially since the mid-19th century, is insatiable. It sees greater government as the greater good. It views individual liberty as dangerous and personal choice – always excepting abortion, the only sacrament the atheist left acknowledges and honors – as contrary to the will of the *demos*. It is always in favor of centralized fascism, including but not limited to the power to ban, criminalize, and anathematize speech and ideas with which it does not agree and which threaten its hegemony.

And all of this in disguise – under the cloak of "compassion," of "tolerance," of "fairness." The Tarnhelm beneath which modern "liberalism" (its very name mocks the political origins of the term) lurks, coiled and ready to strike whenever our side lets down its guard. "Come, I think hell's a fable," says Dr. Faustus to Mephistopheles in Marlowe's play. "Ay, think so still, till experience change thy mind," replies the devil. And so in the hell the left has made of America over the past half-century or so we currently dwell.

How did we get here? How have we wandered so far afield from the founding virtues of individualism, self-reliance, bootstrapism, private (as opposed to public) charity, religious belief, religious liberty, personal expression, freedom of both public and private speech, the Judeo-Christian heritage, the right to self-defense? What Mephistophelian toxin has been injected into our body politic, the kind that makes us first doubt, then reject, and then finally mock our own first principles? With America teetering on the brink of collapse for the first time since perhaps the War of 1812, how do we combat, overthrow, and finally eradicate the scourge of "liberalism" – which

With America teetering on the brink of collapse for the first time since perhaps the War of 1812, how do we combat, overthrow, and finally eradicate the scourge of "liberalism"?

in its modern incarnation has nothing to do with classical liberalism – from our national dialogue?

The first step is to overcome our innate squeamishness about the nature of the task at hand. In order to defeat existential evil, one must not only give the devil his due but also use his own weapons against him. No doctor seeks accommodation with cancer. No general seeks to give a defeated mortal enemy a sense of self-esteem – not to mention the hope of victory. As we learned during the victorious wars of our national history, "defeat" should not be temporary but permanent: Nazi Germany and Imperial Japan will never again rise, nor the Confederacy. Until the right learns this lesson and acts on its implications – in the words of Ted "Chappaquiddick" Kennedy – "the work goes on, the cause endures, the hope still lives, and the dream shall never die."

Alas, their dream is our nightmare. In order to defeat the left – having now exchanged its carnival mask of "liberalism" for (once more) "progressivism" – we must halt the work, stifle the cause, annihilate the hope, and bury the dream. To do otherwise is to condemn posterity to endless battle.

Observe a current electoral map. The so-called red states (and how did the socialist left saddle the American right with the color of Communism? You can thank the broadcast networks) overwhelmingly represent the fly-over heartland. It's the country of the artless hello, of low taxes, low unemployment, and low dependency – the country of unlocked doors, personal honesty, moral standards, and the handshake after which you don't have to count your fingers. The blue states, on the other hand, represent the party of Big Government; high taxes; higher incomes (mostly derived from government, academe, or Hollywood, which is to say from taxpayers or suckers); proud chicanery; public-employees' unions; the corrupt Democratic big-city machines in Chicago, Kansas City, St. Louis, San Francisco, and elsewhere; flimflam; three-card monte; and a tradition of fleecing the marks – who, after all, have it coming.

Whose side would you rather be on? To answer that question – honestly – is to declare your allegiance in the Cold Civil War. A war in which every man's hand is against every other man's, in which the battle is not being fought over slavery or states' rights but over the most fundamental principles of the Republic:

> *We hold these truths to be self-evident, that all men are created equal, that they are endowed by their Creator with certain unalienable Rights, that among these are Life, Liberty and the pur-*

suit of Happiness. — That to secure these rights,
Governments are instituted among Men, deriv-
ing their just powers from the consent of the
governed, — That whenever any Form of Gov-
ernment becomes destructive of these ends, it is
the Right of the People to alter or to abolish it,
and to institute new Government, laying its
foundation on such principles and organizing
its powers in such form, as to them shall seem
most likely to effect their Safety and Happiness.

And yet who knew that less than a decade after the founding, Americans would already be debating the wisdom of the founders? Let the indictment proceed.

Burr, Hamilton, and Original Sin

Aaron Burr Jr. — the third vice president of the United States — is today a largely misremembered figure, especially on the left, and for good reason. Overshadowed in his treachery by Benedict Arnold (who, like Burr, had been an officer in the Continental Army), the New Jersey-born Burr avoided the disgraced

Arnold's ultimate self-exile to London, spending some years in that city – mostly fleeing creditors – before his return to Manhattan (by tradition, the most seditious city in the Union) and his eventual death in Staten Island, burial in his hometown of Princeton, and resurrection as the revisionist hero of a Gore Vidal novel.

But let's give credit where credit is due. Burr, one of the founders of the Democratic Party – called Democratic-Republicans back then – not only arguably murdered (there is some evidence that Hamilton, who got off the first shot, fired into the ground) the first treasury secretary of the United States but also went on to establish the *fons et origo* of American municipal corruption, Tammany

---

If there's one thing the Democrats hate, it's war – unless, of course, they start one.

Hall. If one man besides George Washington can be said to have set the American experiment on its future course – in this case not for good but for ill – that man is Burr. Most important, the duel ended with the destruction of the Federalists and ultimately the Whigs, who succeeded the Federalists as the opposition party. It also, in its own lethal way, fixed the notion of the adversarial two-party system in the American psyche – even if it meant that the Democrats literally had to kill off the opposition.

The fatal confrontation of 1804 in Weehawken, N.J., was the culmination of a bitter personal and political animosity between Burr and Hamilton, which included the hotly contested election of 1800, in which Hamilton's vote was crucial in denying Burr the presidency in favor of Thomas Jefferson. But it was more than that. It was the embodiment of the struggle between the Federalists of Washington, Adams, and Hamilton and the Democratic-Republicans of Jefferson and Burr – a struggle that, in one form or another (and with sides changing from time to time), has been going on ever since.

And did Burr suffer any meaningful penalty for killing Hamilton, even though dueling was outlawed in both New York and New Jersey? Of course not – he was, after all, a Democrat. Indicted for murder in both states, he skated in both jurisdictions. In fact, he continued as Jefferson's vice president to the end of the first term. Right from the start, Democrats learned how to game the legal system.

Jefferson was a great president. His fights with the other founders were over means, not ends; they were all patriots who surely would have hanged together had they lost the Revolution. But the party went the way of Burr, not Jefferson. In fact, Burr doubled down on criminality. Tammany Hall evolved into the gold standard in big-city, machine-politics corruption. If slavery was the original sin of the 13 colonies, then Tammany and its imitative ilk in other big cities was the original sin of the Republic: politics as factionalism, special-interest groups, and legalized bribery.

During the election of 1828, Tammany threw its support to Andrew Jackson, creating the spoils system and cementing its relationship with the modern Democratic Party to this day.

WHIGS, COPPERHEADS, AND THE GREAT CIVIL WAR

If there's one thing the Democrats hate, it's war – unless, of course, they start one. And if there's one thing they hate even more than war, it's a war fought for bedrock constitutional principles – in other words, a war fought against everything they believe in. And the Civil War, led by the first Republican president, Abraham Lincoln, could not have illustrated that more clearly.

The Republican Party was formed as an explicitly antislavery party (as opposed to the slavery party, which was the you-know-whos) in the wake of the Whigs' collapse, as that party was torn asunder over the "peculiar institution." In the election of 1856, the Republican candidate, John C. Frémont, vehemently opposed the expansion of slavery under the Kansas-Nebraska Act, which allowed settlers to vote whether to allow slavery. The party's slogan was "Free Soil, Free Labor, Free Speech, Free Men, and Frémont." Who could be against that?

Naturally, the Democrats were. Frémont lost to Democrat James A. Buchanan, whose party had invented the Kansas-Nebraska Act; the third-party candidate in the race – and the last gasp of the Whigs, who had fractured over the expansion of slavery into the territories – was former President Millard Fillmore, who represented the anti-Catholic Know-Nothing Party. As president, Fillmore had signed the Fugitive Slave Act of 1850, which held that runaway slaves had to be returned to the masters, a law upheld seven years later in the infamous *Dred Scott* decision by the Supreme Court under Democratic (of course) Chief Justice Roger B. Taney. The Democrats' problem with race would only worsen over the years.

During the Civil War, the Army of the

> *The Democrats have consistently championed class envy, social division, and often – quite nakedly – racism, if they thought it would buy them votes.*

Potomac was led by the cautious yet resolutely insubordinate George B. McClellan, who consistently managed to be outmaneuvered by Robert E. Lee, commanding the Army of Northern Virginia, even when McClellan had numerical and tactical superiority – as during the Peninsula Campaign. "If he can't fight himself, he excels in making others ready to fight," said Lincoln, who eventually fired him.

McClellan, who had finished second in his class at West Point and never suffered from a deficit of self-esteem, sought payback in the election of 1864, when he ran against his former commander in chief as a Democrat.

His party platform had been written by the antiwar, borderline seditious Copperheads, northern "peace" Democrats who denounced Lincoln as a tyrant and advocated a negotiated settlement with the South. With victory over the Confederacy in sight, Lincoln won with 55 percent of the vote, including the lion's share of the military vote. (Republicans named the Copperheads after the venomous snake; today we would simply call them Democrats but still keep the snake.)

A few months later, President Lincoln was murdered by a Democrat, John Wilkes Booth.

THE SOCIETY OF ST. TAMMANY, GANGLAND, AND THE LITTLE TIN BOX

The Democratic Party has always appealed to the basest instincts of the American people, molting and changing shape as the political winds dictated but solely devoted to its raison d'être: the accumulation and retention of political power. As it evolved over the course of the late 19th century, its chief mechanism became, in essence, bribery – not simply of civil officials but of the public itself.

It's unclear who said, "A Democracy cannot exist as a permanent form of government. It can only last until the citizens discover they can vote themselves largesse out of the public treasury." But that may as well be the party's animating ethos: "social justice" disguised as sympathy or, worse, compassion. Always wrapping itself in the false cloak of righteousness and celebrating the folk wisdom of the *demos*, the Democrats have consistently championed class envy, social division, and often – quite nakedly – racism, if they thought it would buy them votes.

Only the Democrats could reinvent themselves so effortlessly, molting from the party of the Ku Klux Klan to the party of the Civil Rights Act of 1964. From the party of the aggressive atheist Madalyn Murray O'Hair, who destroyed school prayer and helped set the country on its downward moral spiral in 1963, to the party of Bible-toting Baptist presidents (Bill Clinton) and the racist ravings of Obama's pastor, the Rev. Jeremiah Wright. When your only principle is power, it's easy to embrace flexibility and nuance.

This amoral relativism raised to a high art

Even today, the State Department remains the most consistently left-wing, at times anti-American, entity in the executive branch.

---

of hypocrisy – for such it is – at the party's core has long posed the most potent threat to its continuing existence; therefore, it is the one aspect of its nature that must be most assiduously concealed and obscured.

And obscure that it has, beginning with the rise of Burr's own Society of St. Tammany, the Democratic Party's political machine in New York City in the mid-19th century. Forget the notorious Boss Tweed, whose reign of blatant corruption finally became too egregious for even New Yorkers to stomach; it was only after his conviction in 1873 that things really got rolling, thanks to the Irish, whom the Tammany nativists had once despised. A series of grand sachems – beginning with "Honest John" Kelly and continuing through the magnificently corrupt reign of Richard "Boss" Croker (who retired to a horse farm in his native Ireland, leaving an estate valued at more than $3 million) and Charles F. Murphy – kept both the votes and the swag flowing. Murphy's private dining room upstairs at the ultra-fashionable Delmonico's restaurant was dubbed the Scarlet Room of Mystery by the New York newspapers, and from it he ruled New York City politics from 1902 to his death in 1924.

In the era of the Little Tin Box, the quiet man was king. Setting the Democrats fully on their strategic path of political tribalism, Tammany assembled a coalition of the dispossessed and the avaricious, of patronage hounds, labor leaders, and various ethnic groups – principally, the newly arrived Irish, Italians, and Jews.

One job open to the toughest gangland chieftains – such as the legendary Monk Eastman, a feared thug who, improbably, later became a war hero – was that of "sheriff" in various bars and dives known as blind pigs or blind tigers. The sheriff controlled crime and violence on his turf (in Eastman's case, part of the Lower East Side) and got out the vote when elections rolled around. His boys pitched in as *shtarkers* – sluggers – who clubbed the opposition's voters into submission at the polls. Meanwhile, other gang members voted two, three, and four times via the simple expedient of shaving off first their side whiskers, then their chin whiskers, and finally their mustaches.

To be fair, Tammany's outreach to the immigrant communities was exemplary. George Washington Plunkitt, a distinguished sachem whose impromptu memoir, *Plunkitt of Tammany Hall* – Plunkitt's wit and wisdom as recorded by William Riordan, a journalist of the day – describes the people skills of your basic Tammany pol:

Big Tom Foley, leader of the Second District, fits in exactly, too. Tom sells whisky, and good whisky, and he is able to take care of himself against a half dozen thugs if he runs up against them on Cherry Hill or in Chatham Square. Pat Ryder and Johnnie Ahearn of the Third and Fourth Districts are just the men for the places. Ahearn's constituents are about half Irishmen and half Jews. He is as popular with one race as with the other. He eats corned beef and kosher meat with equal nonchalance, and it's all the same to him whether he takes off his hat in the church or pulls it down over his ears in the synagogue.

There was a lot to be said for the wigwam's way, and in fact its system of patronage and kickbacks, of favors asked and received, elevated a sizable proportion of the immigrants out of their ghettos and into the middle class. The Irish rabble slowly transformed into the backbone of the city's police force and legal community (William J. Fallon, the most flamboyant defense attorney of his day, was known as the Great Mouthpiece – he never lost a homicide beef); the Jews, who briefly dominated violent crime in the 1920s and early '30s, overcame institutional discrimination and sent their kids to Harvard and other Ivy League schools; the Italians, last off the boat, were electing mayors and governors within a couple of generations.

Indeed, the Roaring '20s and the Depression '30s were probably the closest the modern Democratic Party has come to doing well by doing good. Tammany and its big-city machine imitators in Chicago, Kansas City, and elsewhere brazenly opposed the GOP "goo-goo" (good government) types. As the unapologetic Alderman Paddy Bauler famously said in 1955, "Chicago ain't ready for reform," and after generations of mayors named Daley, it still ain't.

Indeed, the Roosevelt years were probably as close as the Democrats ever came to a workable electoral model. The country rallied around FDR twice, first during the Depression and later during the war. Roosevelt got elected four times for a reason, and not simply because the nation had rejected

---

All the strains of modern "progressivism" are present in Obama: the hostility toward the country as founded and the mad desire to hobble the country's future via taxation, regulation, and executive order.

Hoover and the GOP. FDR gave the country hope in the worst of economic times – even if his Big Government nostrums largely continued the failed philosophy of the previous administration and his statist inclinations recalled Wilson's – and promised ultimate, unconditional-surrender victory over the Axis. It was a promise he delivered on, even if he did not live to actually see it.

But the introduction of Big Labor into the Tammany/gangland mix would prove exceedingly harmful to the party's moral center. Although they are less well known today than their more flamboyant colleagues such as Lucky Luciano and Dutch Schultz, two pivotal figures in the transformation of the modern Democratic Party into a full-blown criminal enterprise were the murderous Louis "Lepke" Buchalter and his muscle partner, Jacob "Gurrah" Shapiro, who not only were instrumental in the founding of Murder Inc. (a Brooklyn-based alliance of Italian and Jewish gunsels) but also took over the garment-district unions. The legalized shakedown rackets we call the public sector unions today, such as the Service Employees International Union (SEIU), are the spiritual sons and heirs of Lepke and Gurrah, except it is the public they now bleed, not just private employers.

Gangland's code of coercion was a system

that worked in its own way, but it came with a soul-corroding price. Even as Hollywood films of the period – especially those from Warner Bros., which are practically gangland documentaries (particularly *The Roaring Twenties* with James Cagney and Humphrey Bogart) – always ended with the moral that crime doesn't pay, real life spoke differently. And not just Boss Croker, hying himself back to the Ould Sod with the contents of his Little Tin Box, but a veritable rogue's gallery of corrupt cops, judges, politicians, mayors, and governors. Everybody, it seems, was either on the take or on the lam.

Let a couple of examples suffice. The first is Aaron J. Levy, a lifelong Tammany hack who was first the Democratic majority leader of the New York State Assembly and then state Supreme Court judge, who protected gambling clubs belonging to Arnold Rothstein and then, after "The Brain's" untimely demise in 1928, continued to shield prominent gangland figures from the bench.

Prominent among them was Owney Madden,

a British-born Irish immigrant who was king of Prohibition New York: brewer of Madden's No. 1 beer; Mae West's lover and Broadway angel; owner of five heavyweight champions of the world, including Primo Carnera and James J. Braddock; and the founder of the Cotton Club, which employed Duke Ellington, Harold Arlen, and Lena Horne. Madden "retired" in Bill Clinton's hometown of Hot Springs, Ark., and died in 1965, having run the spa city known affectionately as Bubbles as his personal fiefdom for 30 years.

It's Madden who leads directly to a more famous figure, Herbert H. Lehman, the former governor of New York and, later, a U.S. senator. Lehman succeeded Franklin Roosevelt in Albany after FDR defeated Hoover, so he was well acquainted with the cozy relationship between the New York underworld and the upstate bonzes in Albany. Lehman himself had a squeaky-clean reputation – and yet when Madden needed a huge favor, he paid off like a slot machine.

When Madden's brother Martin, a British subject who, unlike Owney, had never bothered to get himself naturalized, was threatened with deportation in 1954, Lehman joined Arkansas Senator John McClellan to co-sponsor a Senate bill, S. 541, which was ratified in June 1955. Favors given and favor received. As Thomas E. Dewey, then the Lehman-appointed special prosecutor in charge of busting up gangland, said of Democrat-dominated Hot Springs in the 1930s, "The whole crowd are a complete ring: the chief of police, the chief of detectives, the mayor and the city attorney." No wonder they called Hot Springs "Tammany South."

Eight decades later, Dewey might make the same observation about the United States of America.

Spies, Marxists, and Barack Hussein Obama

With the waning of Tammany power in the 1950s and the beginning of the Cold War, the price of Democratic corruption suddenly ratcheted up as national security came into play. During World War II, the Soviet Union had been busily placing penetration agents at high levels in the American government. Under a top-secret initiative run from Moscow called the Illegals Program, the Soviets managed to infiltrate American-born agents into the war effort and the administration during the Democrats' long reign from 1933 to 1953.

One such agent was George Koval, an Iowa-born scientist who was perhaps the Soviet Union's most effective atomic spy. Koval's radical Russian-born Jewish parents had come to Sioux City from a shtetl near Minsk but returned to the USSR in 1932, to Stalin's "Jewish Autonomous Region" of Birobidzhan. Recruited by the GRU (Soviet military intelligence), Koval was sent back to the U.S., where he looted secrets from the Manhattan Project labs in Oak Ridge and Dayton. The year after his leisurely 1948 return to Moscow, during the Truman administration, the Soviets exploded their first bomb. Koval's existence wasn't revealed until 2006, the year he died in obscurity at age 92.

Even more important was the Soviet agent Harry Dexter White, a senior Treasury Department official under FDR, whose perfidy was exposed by the Venona cables – intercepted Soviet transmissions that revealed the extent of Communist penetration. What seems today a cavalier disregard for security was the result of our wartime alliance with Stalin, but it had significant repercussions for American foreign policy under Truman (the Alger Hiss case), Eisenhower, and Kennedy. Senator Joseph McCarthy wasn't crazy after all: There really were spies in the State Department. Lots of them. Even today, State remains the most consistently left-wing, at times anti-American, entity in the executive branch.

Take the case of "Agent 202," Walter Kendall Myers, a State Department analyst who in 2010 received a life sentence for spying on behalf of Cuba for 30 years. Unrepentant to the end, Myers and his wife, Gwendolyn (who had once been a legislative aide to former Democratic Senator James Abourezk in her native South Dakota), told U.S. District Court Judge Reggie Walton that "we acted as we did because of our ideals and beliefs. We did not act out of anger – or out of any anti-Americanism. Our overriding objective was to help the Cuban people defend their revolution."

The Myerses sold out their country for love: the worst and most dangerous kind of spies. But the fact is, a significant segment of the left sees absolutely nothing wrong with what they did. Traitors like the Myerses and the Rosenbergs can justify their treachery by appealing to what the left likes to call a "higher morality." An unearned, bogus moral superiority justifies, in their minds, any actions they take against their own country – which, after all, is to blame for the parlous state of the world.

And that's because on the left, there has always been considerable sympathy for

Marxist ideas and ideals. Koval came by his naturally; others, like Hiss, gravitated to them; and the Myerses went looking for them. But something in Marxism, Communism, and – especially, I would argue – totalitarianism fires the imagination of the "peaceful and tolerant" left, which can't wait to seize power and impose its will on the citizens of the United States – for their own good, naturally.

And yet many, particularly on the left, play down intelligence operations directed against the U.S. Writing in *The Wall Street Journal* in April 2012, Michelle Van Cleave, the chief of U.S. counterintelligence under George W. Bush, noted Vice President Joe Biden's flippant attitude toward ongoing Russian espionage, then remarked, "The vice president may be surprised to learn that there are as many Russian intelligence officers operating in the U.S. today as during the height of the Cold War – it is arrests and criminal proceedings that have fallen off." For the former Soviets, the Principal Enemy remains, well, the Principal Enemy – and the

Obama administration remains willfully blind. Even when in 2010 it actually caught some illegals – including the 10-member ring of the fetching Anna Chapman – it hustled them back to Russia before any useful intelligence could be extracted from them.

But then that's to be expected under a Democratic administration, especially one as socialist-friendly as Barack Obama's. For Obama is the ne plus ultra of the twin strains of anti-American leftist thought, the spawn of the gangster ethos of the 1920s and '30s and the fashionable Marxism of the "revolutionary" year of 1968, which gave birth to the George McGovern candidacy in 1972 and has been waiting – like the Shiites for the Twelfth Imam – for its next messiah ever since. All the strains of modern "progressivism" are present in the president: the hostility toward the country as founded ("fundamental change") and the mad desire to hobble the country's future via taxation, regulation, and executive order. The Columbia-educated Obama is the living embodiment of the

Columbia-born Cloward-Piven strategy, the word made flesh and dwelling among us, practicing a "progressive," American form of *taqiyya* in order to conceal his real, ideologically inimical intentions.

EACH DAWN I DIE,
Jake Lingle, and the Way Forward

Despite – or perhaps because of – their great triumph in 2008, the Democrats are today faced with a new dilemma: how to hang onto their gains. For the modern left, electoral victories are now subject to an American version of the old Brezhnev Doctrine. That relic of the Soviet Union decreed that once a country went Communist, it could never return to the old ways. (The same is true of territories conquered by Islam, which may be one reason why the totalitarian left is so fond of the Mohammedans, ideologically speaking.)

And so they redouble their dance with the thing what brung them: Tammany Hall and its proud history of voter fraud. Note how fiercely the Democrats fight laws requiring citizens to produce some form of government-issued identification in order to vote. Without the crucial element of inner-city voting "irregularities" in places like Philadelphia, St. Louis, and Seattle, their holds on Pennsylvania, Missouri, and even Washington State would be seriously weakened.

Thus – by any means necessary – they continue to steal elections, discovering new ballots (Seattle, 2004); simply printing as many new ballots as needed to make up a deficit (Bridgeport, Conn., 2010); or getting pet judges to keep polling places open after hours (St. Louis, 2000).

Lefties like to claim – based on zero evidence – that there's no proof of actual voter fraud, as opposed to registration fraud, which even they can't pretend doesn't exist. But it goes beyond merely voting. In April 2012, four Democratic officials in Indiana were charged with felonies for allegedly faking petition signatures for Obama and Hillary Clinton – enough to put them on the ballot.

Obama went on to squeak out a November win in Indiana, but it's an open question whether he ever should have been on the ballot in the first place.

Didn't know that? That's because, despite the rise of the Internet and talk radio, most

---

The American media remain resolutely "progressive" and Democratic – more so now than at any time in the past half-century.

Americans still get what passes for news from the MSM (the mainstream media, AKA the "legacy media"). Although printed newspapers will soon be a thing of the past, they still survive, along with their visual counterparts, the dinosaur broadcast networks.

And despite their pro forma denials, the American media remain resolutely "progressive" and Democratic – more so now than at any time in the past half-century. The reasons are not conspiratorial. Just as liberals have taken over academe and Hollywood, so also have they commandeered the media, because – unlike conservatives – they naturally gravitate toward those professions. Like the civil-rights movement in the decade before it, the Watergate scandal of 1972–74 energized journalism, attracting those amateur evangelists who wanted to "make a difference" and who might otherwise have gone into, say, the law.

The problem is, reporters are supposed to report – not make a difference. The American news business now more closely resembles the frankly partisan European media than it does, say, the old *New York Times* of Mike Berger, Abe Rosenthal, and Harold C. Schonberg. Today, however, reporters conceal more than they report. It is, for example, something of a parlor game on the right to play "Name That Party," an amusement that spontaneously occurs whenever a Democratic politician or public figure is caught with his hand in the cookie jar: Almost never will the left-leaning media provide his party affiliation in their accounts.

Worse, reporters have uncritically adopted the Marxist tone and vocabulary of the left ("social justice," "gender inequality"). They've been steeped in the brew of leftism, if not from birth, then certainly from education, so it's no wonder that Obama in 2008 was the beneficiary of the most adoring, uncritical press in American political history. It wasn't that the reporters didn't want to know about the president's obscure past: his parents, his upbringing, his college years, his grades, his employment history, all the stuff of normal "human interest" stories. It's just that the signal aspect of his candidacy – that he would be the First Black President – outweighed their fiduciary duty toward their employers and the American public.

Today's journalists are only too happy to protect a compromised pol – think Teddy Kennedy – as long as he's on the "right" side of the issues. For them, the struggle between ends and means always results in favor of the

ends. (In a pair of 2012 blog posts, two prominent writers for *The New York Times*, Stanley
Fish and Andrew Rosenthal, more or less said
this openly.) Favored targets are business-
men, not Democratic government officials;
with Obama in office, all Washington is a skat-

---

*Today, a "Scoop Jackson
Democrat" — socially liberal but
strong on defense — is as extinct
as his namesake.*

---

ing rink on which characters like Barney Frank
and Chris Dodd turn triple lutzes while their
media cronies applaud like the Harvard-
trained seals many of them are.

Today, following the lead of David Axel-
rod, the former *Chicago Tribune* reporter
turned wealthy Democratic campaign con-
sultant and adviser to President Obama,
reporters play both sides of the street in the

hopes of striking it rich. Like the fence Mr. Peachum in *The Beggar's Opera*, they act "both against Rogues and for 'em." With a little luck, they can hope to escape the demeaning drudgery of journalism and become the White House press secretary, the head of the Aspen Institute, or a deputy secretary of state.

In other words, they've all become Jake Lingle, the corrupt *Tribune* legman who made an illicit fortune covering the Capone mob for Colonel McCormick's broadsheet while at the same time working for Scarface Al himself. One day in 1930, while crossing under Michigan Avenue on his way to the train and the racetrack down in Homewood, a gunman put a Colt Detective Special .38 – gangland's weapon of choice – behind his ear and pulled the trigger. Jake died with his cigar still smoldering in his mouth, which ought to be a cautionary tale but hasn't been.

Locked in an unholy ideological alliance with a criminal organization masquerading as a political party, the media need not wonder how they – representing the American public, on whose behalf they're supposed to operate – got here. All they need to do is keep doing it. Once the ends justify the means, anything goes. When "by any means necessary" is not just a revolution slogan but a philosophy of life, when emotion is prized over reason, and when the icons of the left are Che Guevara and Mao instead of Jefferson and FDR, then all power really does flow from the barrel of the gun of electoral-power politics.

In Conclusion

For more than two centuries, the Democratic Party has done its best to disguise its real aims. It preached tolerance even as it oppressed immigrants and lynched black people. It spoke of compassion even as it condemned three generations of African Americans to a plantation existence and destroyed their cultural institutions. It "celebrated diversity" not by defining deviancy down (in the late Daniel Patrick Moynihan's memorable phrase) but by elevating and mainstreaming, via journalism and Hollywood, the worst cultural pathologies of the underclass. It constantly agitates for society to drop its squaresville morality and worship at the altar of the only god leftism really honors: the God of Self-Gratification.

In Milton's *Paradise Lost*, Books V and VI, we read the almost throwaway story of the seraph Abdiel who, swayed by Lucifer's tongue, at first dawdles with the insurgents and then realizes his folly and returns to the light. Abdiel is perhaps the most sympathetic character in the poem, a stand-in for weak humanity (though angelic). Listening to Satan, Abdiel rebukes the demon's monstrous lies:

So spake the Seraph Abdiel faithful found,
Among the faithless, faithful only hee;
Among innumerable false, unmov'd,
Unshak'n, unseduc'd, unterrifi'd
His Loyaltie he kept, his Love, his Zeale;
Nor number, nor example with him wrought
To swerve from truth, or change his constant
*   mind*

Though single. From amidst them forth he passd,
Long way through hostile scorn, which he
*   susteind*
Superior, nor of violence fear'd aught;
And with retorted scorn his back he turn'd
On those proud Towrs to swift
destruction doom'd.

After nearly two and half centuries of Democratic political perfidy, cultural malevolence, and, when necessary, sedition and outright treason — and however imperfect the political alternative — is it not time for us to emulate Abdiel and call them what they are? To no longer be seduced by their sweet nothings of tolerance and compassion and fairness and social justice and to instead apply the hard-won realism of our forefathers, who, like Milton, understood man's fallen nature?

The days of patriotic, centrist Democrats like the late Washington State Senator Henry "Scoop" Jackson have been over since the McGovern revolution. Once upon a time, conservative Democrats were in the vanguard

It's time to send the Democrats the way of the Federalists, the Whigs, the Know-Nothings, the Dixiecrats, and the other splinter parties and factions that litter American political history.

of the fight against Communism. Today, a "Scoop Jackson Democrat" – socially liberal but strong on defense – is as extinct as his namesake. Instead the radical left, following their guru, Saul Alinsky (who famously acknowledged Lucifer in his manifesto, *Rules for Radicals*), continues to insist that conservatives are their enemy and that we can be broken by the application of his rule No. 4: "Make the enemy live up to their own book of rules." That any deviation from what the leftist media insists are conservative standards is proof of hypocrisy. Like the aliens in

Independence Day, they're using our satellites – our institutions and our moral code – against us, and for decades their ethos and their arguments carried the day.

No longer. It's time to make them live up to *their* rule book and their moral code, which is to say, no rule book or moral code at all. To expose them for the power-hungry nihilists they have become – the true sons and daughters of Aaron Burr. The minute the American people fully grasp that the modern Democratic Party has become the reductio ad absurdum of itself, the inevitable result of its cynical nihilism, the Democrats' long war against the United States will finally end.

After more than two centuries, it's time to send the Democrats the way of the Federalists, the Whigs, the Know-Nothings, the Dixiecrats, and the other splinter parties and factions that litter American political history. No law says a given political party is eternal. And yet as long as the party of Burr continues to thrive, its loaded gun is no longer pointing at a man but at a whole nation.

Is there a place in the American political system for a truly loyal opposition – one that does not seek "fundamental transformation" of our constitutional Republic but rather its betterment and continuance? Of course there is.

But is there a place for a criminal organization masquerading as a political party?

If our nation is to survive, not any more.

First American edition published in 2012 by Encounter Books, an activity of Encounter for Culture and Education, Inc., a nonprofit, tax exempt corporation.
Encounter Books website address: www.encounterbooks.com

Manufactured in the United States and printed on acid-free paper. The paper used in this publication meets the minimum requirements of ANSI/NISO Z39.48 1992 (R 1997) (*Permanence of Paper*).

FIRST AMERICAN EDITION

LIBRARY OF CONGRESS CATALOGING-IN-PUBLICATION DATA

Walsh, Michael.
The people v. the Democratic Party / by Michael Walsh.
p.   cm.
ISBN 978-1-59403-661-3 (pbk. : alk. paper)
ISBN 978-1-59403-662-0 (ebook)
1. Democratic Party (U.S.)—History. I. Title.
II. Title: People versus the Democratic Party.
JK2316.W36 2012
324.2736—dc23
2012020825

10 9 8 7 6 5 4 3 2 1